**the marquise
stayed in**

STINGRAY CLAPPING
by Andrew Choate © 2012
Insert Blanc Press June 2012

First Paperback Edition June 2016

ISBN: 978-0-9961696-9-1

INSERT
B L A N C
PRESS

Insert Blanc Press
Los Angeles, CA
insertblancpress.net
insertpress@gmail.com

STINGRAY CLAPPING

ANDREW CHOATE

INSERT
BLANC
PRESS

Los Angeles

unsafe upholstery
safe liposuction

pitch thrust carrion

the phrase "your last name"

fingers are for buttons
fingers are buttons
fingers for buttons

necktie popcorn

I don't want to bother you much with what happened to me personally.

more nipple than fig
more fig than nipple
dress up as fig
for Halloween
dress up as
nipple for birthd
figple

your luggage arrived
before you

melee over tile

get the
shoe you
deserve to

thugly, calmly, girls

bathroom shoulders

you can run
but you can't
aquarium

jersey kitten
furball
gag order

a fact
uh fact
hoof act
aif act
aphid
ape fthwack

apron manor

yeah, sure, we understand
loss, but what about
accumulation

frozen ant arkansas
frozen
ant
ark
ansas
frozen ant ark tic ness

scan band aid

body golf

Use computers to research dinosaurs.
Use humans to research computers.

witness biscuit

commitment to advice

covert dreamer hurrumph

compromise a living room

assassinatable fun

karate dinner
karate dance
karate dinner dance

mirepoix Iroquois

What I do

disenchanted by object
relations theory

I am not disclosing any trade secrets.

insert prince here

semiempirical expressions

uhmmmmhmm, so feasible

only the spectres
learn lessons

exuberant subjective
rationalism

I experience a certain
kind of pleasure in
rediscovering, thanks
to these lines, the events
they relate.

we broke for lunch

military secrets
culinary secrets
romantic secrets
technology secrets
family secrets
architectural secrets
educational secrets
military bliss

conscious credit

good will radar check
mate

you can even try baseball

I love bells,
just not those kind.
I love bells.
No, not that kind.

urine garage courtesy

horse by watching

potential commercial
watermelon sale

morale normal

I taste skeleton

love slash utilization

so much for that beverage

this is actually your
old form

rocks and waterfalls
listen
to music

diablo lacunae
crash
accordingly

You know how I make
room for hikers.

coffin feathers